I0476052

Classy Stats

How To Communicate Quantitative Information Effectively

JOSEPH D. KEEFER, PH.D.

CENTER FOR EXCELLENCE
IN ENGLISH USAGE

Chapel Hill, North Carolina

CLASSY STATS

Copyright © 2017 by Joseph D. Keefer

ISBN: 978-1544126746

Classy Stats

Section 1: Guidance on Numbers

Make sure that the data and statistics
you use are credible and up-to-date.   1

Correctly interpret the statistics
that you acquire.   2

Make sure that any calculations   5
you perform are correct.

Present your statistics accurately.   6

Make your statistics meaningful.   12

Present your statistics clearly.   18

Section 2: Guidance on Words

Use statistical terminology correctly.   21

Show that you understand the subtleties
of common words and expressions
used in describing numbers.   28

Write clearly.   34

Write concisely.   37

Section 3: Guidance on Graphics

Make sure that the information contained
in a graphic is correct.   39

In a graphic, provide all of the information
needed for correct interpretation.   41

Avoid producing graphics that can
mislead readers.   42

Structure graphics in ways that make
major statistical findings easy to discern.   43

In your graphics, make the text, numbers
and design elements easy to read.   47

Avoid cluttering your graphics with
numbers that readers do not need.   51

Avoid cluttering your graphics with
distracting or unnecessary design elements. 52

Examples of statistical graphics   58

Introduction

Every day millions of students and professionals face the important task of communicating quantitative information. The book *Classy Stats* is designed to help people accomplish that task more effectively.

Classy Stats is essentially three books in one.

It is a book that will help journalists and other writers who want to become better at understanding and communicating statistics.

It is a book that will help researchers, analysts and statisticians who want to become better at writing about the results of their analyses.

And it is a book that will help anyone who wants to become better at producing basic statistical graphics.

Students and professionals who master the principles presented in *Classy Stats* will find themselves more confident when they are "home alone" working on a major statistics-based project.

In that type of project, a person is expected to produce, with little or no help, an article, report or presentation that demonstrates professional-level skill in the "Big Three"—numbers, words and graphics.

Classy Stats shows people in various fields how to avoid missteps in communicating quantitative information, and the book shows people the "best practices" for communicating quantitative information effectively.

Section 1

Guidance on Numbers

1.1 Make sure that the data and statistics you use are credible and up-to-date.

1.1.1 In your writing, you routinely will need to use statistics that were not produced by you or your organization. Make sure that you acquire those statistics directly from credible sources. For example, government agencies and non-partisan research organizations typically are good sources for objective data on public policy issues. In addition, major issue-advocacy organizations can provide useful research findings promoting a point of view.

1.1.2 Occasionally you will encounter a report or news article that presents an interesting statistic and identifies the source of that statistic. Before using that statistic in your writing, you need to check with the source to verify that the statistic had been correctly reported. Often you can accomplish that task simply by checking the website or publications of the source organization.

1.1.3 If, in your reading, you encounter an interesting statistic for which a source is not listed, do not use that statistic unless you can find the source and verify the statistic.

1.1.4 When you use a statistic in your writing, cite the source of that statistic, unless the statistic is providing information that can be considered common knowledge.

1.1.5 Many statistical measures are updated regularly—measures such as a country's population or a company's earnings. Make sure that you use up-to-date statistics in your writing. To avoid using out-of-date statistics, you should check the website of the organization providing the statistics before you use the statistics.

1.1.6 Perhaps you are preparing a report or presentation for delivery in, say, three months, and you will need to use certain statistics. You should check with the sources of those statistics to determine whether updated statistics might become available before you deliver your report or presentation.

1.2 Correctly interpret the statistics that you acquire.

1.2.1 If the statistic that you are using describes the difference between two percentages, make sure that you express the difference as "percentage points"—not "percent."

For example:

• If 75 percent of students passed a particular test last year and 80 percent passed this year, the increase was 5 percentage points — not 5 percent.

• If 85 percent of the female students taking a test earned a passing grade and 75 percent of the male students passed, the difference between the men and women was 10 percentage points — not 10 percent.

1.2.2 When you describe a number as being an "average," readers will assume that you are referring to a "mean." If the number you are reporting is a "median," then be sure to characterize the number as a "median" — not as an "average."

1.2.3 Be careful when you use numbers that you found displayed in a column within a statistical table or displayed on an axis in a chart or graph. The number displayed might be a shortened form of the actual number. For example, if a column heading includes the notation "000's" or "thousands," you would need to add three zeros to every number in that column before using those numbers.

For example:

If a particular column in a table is labeled "revenue in 000's," that means the number "$3,225" should be read as "$3,225,000" or "$3.225 million."

1.2.4 If you are using a statistic found in a research report, make sure that you know whether the statistic applies to a population or to a sample. A population-based statistic summarizes data collected about every element of a particular set — for example, all 5,000 first-year students at a university. Sample-based statistics summarize data collected about a portion of a population — for example, 500 of those 5,000 students.

1.2.5 If you use a sample-based statistic, you need to state whether people in the sample had been randomly selected. If a random sample was used, researchers can make defensible inferences about the population from which the sample was drawn.

1.2.6 If you are writing about results based on a random sample, you need to report whether the research findings were considered to be statistically significant.

1.2.7 Occasionally you will encounter research based on non-random samples, such as samples comprising people who volunteered to participate in an online poll. Be wary of using statistics based on non-random samples. For results derived from non-random samples, no statistical testing is appropriate.

1.3 Make sure that any calculations that you perform are correct.

1.3.1 Sometimes you may need to perform calculations on your acquired data to produce a new statistical measure. Avoid making careless errors when you perform those calculations—errors such as transposing numbers or putting a decimal point in the wrong place.

1.3.2 When calculating the percentage by which a quantity changed over time, make sure that you use as the denominator the quantity in the earlier year—not the later year.

For example:

If a state's population increased from 5 million in 2000 to 5.5 million in 2015, divide the change—500,000—by 5 million to get a change of 10 percent.

1.3.3 When multiplying a number by a percentage that is less than 1.0, make sure that you use the correct decimal to represent the percentage.

For example:

To calculate 0.75 per cent of $100,000, multiply $100,000 by .0075 – not .75 – to get $750.

1.3.4 When projecting how much an amount will change over time, make sure that you take into account the effect of compounding.

For example:

Assume that the median sale price of homes in a particular community is $250,000, and that real estate leaders project that the median sale price will increase by 5 percent a year in inflation-adjusted dollars in each of the next three years. To estimate the projected median sale price at the end of the three-year period, you need to: (1) multiply $250,000 by 1.05 to get $262,500; (2) multiply $262,500 by 1.05 to get $275,600; and (3) multiply $275,600 by 1.05 to get $289,400. (If you had simply multiplied $250,000 by 1.15, you would have gotten an incorrect estimate of $287,500.) The projected median sale price of $289,400 after three years is 15.8 percent higher than the current price.

1.4 Present your statistics accurately.

1.4.1 Avoid making careless errors when stating a number. For example, do not write "12.5" when you mean "1.25," do not write "12,000" when you mean "120,000," and do not write "million" when you mean "billion."

1.4.2 Be sure to report the correct unit of measurement. For example, do not write "square yards" if you mean "cubic yards," and do not write "pounds" if you mean "tons."

1.4.3 Be alert to differences between metric measurements and U.S. measurements. For example, do not write "miles" when you mean "kilometers" and do not write "grams" when you mean "ounces."

1.4.4 Be alert to the currency in which a sum of money is denominated. For example, do not write "dollars" when you mean "euros."

1.4.5 Be careful when describing the rate at which something happens. For example, do not write "per month" when you mean "per year," and do not write "parts per million" when you mean "parts per billion."

1.4.6 In a ratio, the larger of the two numbers typically is expressed first, as in a 3-to-1 ratio. In describing a ratio, make sure to place the accompanying terms in the correct order.

For example:

If the average number of students per teacher in a school is 20, then you should write that the student-teacher ratio is 20-to-1. It would be incorrect to write "teacher-student ratio."

1.4.7 If the data that you have acquired are in decimal form within a spreadsheet, normally you will need to convert the decimal values to percentages before you present your statistics. Be careful when you do that.

For example:

The decimal value of .03 equals "3 in 100," or 3 percent, but the decimal value of .003 equals "3 in 1,000," or 0.3 percent.

1.4.8 If you report the amount of each part of a whole, make sure that the sum of the parts equals the amount of the whole.

For example:

If a government agency has a budget of $10 million and the budget is divided into four categories, the budgets that you list for the four categories need to sum to $10 million.

1.4.9 If you report the percentage share of each part of a whole, make sure that the sum of the percentages equals 100 percent—or 99 or 101, accounting for rounding. For example, if you wrote that the whole contained three categories having shares of 20 percent, 30 percent and 40 percent, that statement would be inaccurate.

1.4.10 If you are describing how a number has changed over time, do not confuse actual change with relative change. For example, you could accurately report that non-Hispanic whites' share of the U. S. population declined between 2000 and 2015, but it would be inaccurate to write that the non-Hispanic whites' population had declined.

1.4.11 Do not mischaracterize the population to which a particular statistic applies.

For example:

Do not write "100 million people" if you mean "100 million households." Do not write "women under 40" if you mean "married women under 40." Do not write "people over 55" if you mean "people 55 and over."

1.4.12 If you are describing an analysis of a variable that has numerically defined response categories, make sure that you correctly report the range covered by each category. The categories need to be mutually exclusive and collectively exhaustive.

For example:

• You would violate the "mutually exclusive" rule if you reported that the research grouped older adults into the age categories of 55-65, 65-75 and 76-and-older. People aged 65 would fit into two groups.

• You would violate the "collectively exhaustive" rule if you reported that the research grouped older adults into the age categories of 55-64, 66-75 and 76-and-older. People aged 65 would not be included in any group.

1.4.13 Be careful when you apply the terms "doubled" or "tripled" as shorthand to describe a percentage increase. For example, an increase from 60 to 120 would amount to a 100 percent increase, or a doubling of the original number. An increase from 60 to 180 would amount to a 200 percent increase, or a "tripling."

1.4.14 When referring to one number being larger than another number, do not use the "times than" construction, as in "two times larger than" or "three times more than." Using the "times than" construction can confuse your audience. Instead of the "times than" construction, use a construction such as "two times as large as" or "three times as many as." Those constructions are easier to grasp.

For example:

If the question is "What is three times eight?" the answer would be 24. However, if the question is "What number is three times larger than eight?" the answer would be 32. That is because you would start with an eight and then add one eight, a second eight and a third eight.

However, if you asked "What number is three times as large as eight?" the answer would be 24. The expression "three times as large as eight" means the same as "three times eight."

1.4.15 When referring to one number being smaller than another number, do not use the constructions "times less than" or "times smaller than" or "times less likely." Those constructions are nonsensical. A number cannot decrease by more than one time, just as a number cannot decrease by more than 100 percent.

For example:

If Texas has 28 million residents and Arizona has 7 million residents, you could write that "Texas has four times as many people as Arizona" or that "Arizona has one-fourth as many people as Texas." However, it would be incorrect to write: "Arizona's population is four times smaller than Texas' population."

1.4.16 If you report that a group contains a particular number of people and if you want to subsequently identify those people, make sure that the number of people identified equals the number you reported as being in the group. For example, if you wrote that eight students had been honored at a ceremony, then the list of students needs to contain eight names.

1.5 Make your statistics meaningful.

1.5.1 When describing the percentage of a whole, state the quantity on which the percentage is based, unless the approximate base number is common knowledge. A large percentage can equal a small quantity, whereas a small percentage can equal a large quantity.

For example:

- 80 percent of 5 equals 4.

- 1 percent of 1 million equals 10,000.

1.5.2 If you mention the percentage-point difference between two percentages, state the percentages that are involved. Depending on the context, a 2-percentage-point increase from 2 percent to 4 percent might be more important than a 2-percentage-point increase from 22 percent to 24 percent.

1.5.3 Mention the share of the whole represented by a particular quantity if that information would help readers.

For example:

• If 8,000 people voted in an election in a city that has 40,000 registered voters, you should state that the 8,000 voters constituted 20 percent of the registered voters.

• If you are a journalist describing a company's plans to close a manufacturing plant employing 700 people, you should: (1) use a government agency website to determine the total number of jobs in the county where the plant is situated; and (2) mention the percentage of total jobs represented by the 700 lost jobs.

1.5.4 Describe how a quantity has changed over time if that information would help readers. If you refer to a percentage change, provide at least one of the numbers on which the percentage change is based.

For example:

Write: "The company reported a $305 million profit in 2016, up 8 percent from 2015."

1.5.5 Describe how a rate or proportion has changed over time if that information would help readers.

For example:

Write: "Hispanics comprised 18 percent of the U.S. population in 2015, up from 13 percent in 2000. "

1.5.6 When describing how a number or a percentage has changed over time, make sure that you state the time period involved.

For example:

Write: "The university's undergraduate enrollment has increased by 1,800 students, or 10 percent, over the past 10 years."

1.5.7 When referring to a percentage increase over time, make sure that you describe the increase in terms of quantity as well as percentage. Otherwise, readers may be misled if the quantities are small.

For example:

Assume that a small city had one murder in 2015 and two in 2016. You could write that the number of murders had doubled, but in that same paragraph you would need to state that the number of murders had increased from one to two.

1.5.8 When referring to an increase in the probability that something will occur, make sure that you describe the increase in terms of quantity as well as percentage. Otherwise, readers may be misled if the quantities are small.

For example:

Assume that as a result of a particular change in air quality, the number of people expected to contract a certain disease will increase from 1-in-a-million to 2-in-a-million. You could write that the risk will double, but in that same paragraph you would need to state that the number had increased from 1-in-a-million to 2-in-a-million.

1.5.9 Mention how a particular person or group compares with peers on a particular measurement if that information would help readers.

For example:

• Describe how a company's profit margin, expressed as a percentage, compares with the industry average.

• Describe how the average test score of students in a particular school district compares with statewide and national averages for the same test.

1.5.10 Mention how the characteristics or performance of a particular person or group compares with a certain standard if that information would help readers.

For example:

• "In our state, 30 percent of adults are considered to be obese, based on federal standards."

1.5.11 When describing how often something occurs in populations of various sizes, use a "per capita" measurement or a "per 100,000 population" measurement.

For example:

Assume that City A, with a population of 2 million, had 160 murders last year. Assume that City B, with a population of 500,000, had 80 murders last year. City A had twice as many murders as City B, but the murder rate for City A was only 8 per 100,000 population, half the rate of 16 per 100,00 population for City B.

1.5.12 When describing how a dollar amount has changed over time, make sure that you take inflation into account.

For example:

If the budget for a particular government agency was $10 million in the year 2010 and $11 million in 2016, the agency's budget has clearly grown in "nominal dollars." However, if you use an inflation-adjustment calculator available on the website of the U. S. Bureau of Labor Statistics, you will find that the $10 million in 2010 is equivalent to $11 million in 2016. Thus, in "real dollars," the agency's budget has not grown.

1.5.13 Report the "median" value of a set of numbers—not the "mean"—if the set contains extremely high or extremely low values. Extreme values can result in a mean that does not accurately reflect the distribution of the numbers within the set.

For example:

For example, the median typically is used in reporting levels of household income. If the median U. S. household income is found to be $54,000, then half of the households earn more than $54,000 and half of the households earn less than $54,000.

1.6 Present your statistics clearly.

1.6.1 Use a comma to separate three-digit units within a large number. For example, write 49,733,422—not 49733422.

1.6.2 Except for stock prices, use decimal units, not fractions, in expressing precise amounts larger than 1, as in "1.25." When referring to amounts of less than 1, spell out the fraction, as in "one-fourth."

1.6.3 Normally, in the text of a report or in a presentation, you should round a percentage to the nearest whole number. If the first decimal attached to a percentage is 5 or more, round up. Otherwise, round down. For example, 57.25 percent becomes 57 percent. Use one or more decimal units with a percentage only when small differences are important or when rounding would exaggerate differences. For example, if you were describing an increase from 5.4 percent to 5.6 percent, retain the decimal unit.

1.6.4 Normally, in the text of a report or in a presentation, you should round numbers in the millions or higher to the whole number or to one decimal place. Use the longer version of a number only when precise measurements are standard or when small differences are important or when rounding would exaggerate differences. For example, 49,670,222 can become 49.7 million or 50 million.

1.6.5 Do not multiply a rounded number by another rounded number. For example, assume that the original numbers to be multiplied were 3,450,000 and 5.65 percent. Multiplying those numbers would give you a result of 194,925. However, if you had rounded the numbers to 3.5 million and 5.7 percent before multiplying, the result would have been 199,500 — a less accurate amount.

1.6.6 If you are presenting research findings in an academic journal or at an academic conference, display the number of decimal units prescribed by the relevant journal or organization.

1.6.7 When, in any writing, you express a percentage that is less than 1, place a zero to the left of the decimal point for the sake of clarity. For example, write "0.3 percent" — not ".3 percent."

1.6.8 Use precise language in describing the range between two numbers in the millions or higher. For example, write that a certain amount is "between $5 million and $7 million"–not "between $5 and $7 million."

1.6.9 Use precise language in describing the difference between two percentages. For example, write: "Our market share has increased from 22 percent to 28 percent"—not "from 22 to 28 percent."

1.6.10 When you are comparing proportions of a whole, do not confuse readers by using fractions containing different denominators. For example, do not write: "Among the favorites in the poll, Brown received one-third of the votes, Greene one-fourth and Redd one-fifth." Instead, use percentages, such as 34 percent for Brown, 26 percent for Greene and 19 percent for Redd.

1.6.11 When describing a particular amount of American currency, use the dollar symbol, followed by the amount, and do not use the word "dollars." For example, write "$44 million" — not "44 million dollars" or "$44 million dollars." Write "$1 million"—not "a million dollars." For other currencies, proceed similarly.

1.6.12 If you use statistics derived from a survey, provide essential information about the survey, including who sponsored the survey, how and when the survey was conducted, how many people were surveyed, what types of people were surveyed, how the people surveyed were selected and the margin of error for the reported results.

Section 2

Guidance on Words

2.1 Use statistical terminology correctly.

2.1.1
correlated

When referring to certain variables being *correlated* with each other, you need to specify whether the variables are "positively correlated" or "negatively correlated." Simply stating that the variables are "correlated" can confuse readers.

Variables are positively correlated if one variable tends to increase when the other variable increases. For example, income is positively correlated with education. Variables that are positively correlated are viewed as exhibiting a "direct relationship."

Variables are negatively correlated if one variable tends to increase when the other variable decreases. For example, the committing of crimes is negatively correlated with education. Variables that are negatively correlated are viewed as having an "inverse relationship."

On another matter, do not confuse "correlation" and "causation." The fact that two variables are correlated does not mean that a change in one variable causes a change in the other variable.

2.1.2
exponential

Exponential is a technical term that means an ever-increasing rate of growth, as in 5 percent the first year, 7 percent the second year and 10 percent the third year. Do not use *exponential* to mean simply "large" and do not use *exponentially* to mean simply "rapidly."

2.1.3
geometric

Geometric is a technical term that refers to a progression that has a constant ratio between successive numbers, as in 2, 4, 8, 16 and 32. Do not use *geometric* to mean simply "large" and do not use *geometrically* to mean simply "rapidly."

2.1.4
inflation

Inflation refers to an increase in the price of goods and services. Thus, inflation itself does not rise or fall. It is the rate of inflation that rises and falls. Write: "The rate of inflation has declined this year"—not "Inflation has declined this year."

2.1.5
margin

The *margin* of victory in a competition is the difference between the winning amount and the losing amount. Do not write: "Jones won re-election by a margin of 67 percent to 33 percent." Instead, write: "Jones was re-elected by a 34-percentage-point margin," or "Jones was re-elected by a vote of 67 percent to 33 percent." Do not write: "Jones was re-elected by a 2-to-1 margin." Instead, write: "Jones was re-elected by a 2-to-1 ratio." In business, "margin" refers to the difference between the price and cost of an item.

2.1.6
margin of error

The term *margin of error* is used in describing results of scientifically conducted surveys such as a public opinion poll. Assume that a scientific poll of 1,200 potential voters shows Candidate A with 52 percent of the likely vote and Candidate B with 48 percent. Assume further than the margin of error reported by the pollster is plus or minus 3 percentage points. That means Candidate A's support within the population of potential voters probably is between 49 percent and 55 percent and that Candidate B's support probably is between 45 percent and 51 percent. Because the two ranges of likely voter support overlap, the best course is to write that the candidates are running "about even." If the two ranges do not overlap, then the difference in support for the candidates is considered to be "statistically significant." If the difference is statistically significant, you can write that the poll found one candidate to be "leading" the other.

2.1.7
mean
median
mode

To obtain the *mean* of a set of values, calculate the sum of the values and then divide that sum by the number of values in the set.

To calculate a mean of a series of test scores, for example, add the scores and divide the sum by the number of scores. If the scores were 75, 82, 82, 83, 86, 87 and 93, the mean would be 84.

In an ordered set of values, the *median* is the point at which half of the values are found above and half below. In the example of the seven test scores, the "median" score would be 83. If eight scores had been involved, the median would be calculated by adding the fourth-highest and fifth-highest scores and dividing by two.

The *mode* is the value that appears most often in a set of values. In the example above, the "mode" score would be 82.

2.1.8
odds

Odds are used to express the likelihood that something will happen, but the term *odds* can lead to confusion. For example, assume that in March an economist said that the odds of a recession the following year were 10-to-1. Assume that in October the economist said that the odds had shifted to 20-to-1. That means the odds of a recession have increased or, to put it another way, the likelihood of a recession has decreased. You could write that the odds of a recession have increased, which is true, but some readers might think that you mean the likelihood of a recession has increased. It is better to avoid using the word *odds* in those circumstances and write that the likelihood of a recession "has decreased" or that a recession is considered "less likely."

2.1.9
percent
percentage
percentage point

The word *percent* means "per 100," and the word *percentage* means "share" or "proportion." Use "percentage" – not "percent" – in a construction such as this: "The percentage of students passing the test increased this year."

A number can increase by an infinite percentage—for example, 400 percent. However, a number can decrease by no more than 100 percent.

The difference between two percentages is expressed as a *percentage-point* increase or decrease. For example, if 75 percent of students passed a particular test last year and 80 percent passed this year, the increase was 5 percentage points—not 5 percent.

2.1.10
population
sample

Population and *sample* are common words, but they also are technical terms used in scientific research. For researchers, a *population* constitutes all of the people, animals, organizations, objects or occurrences that are the subject of interest of a particular study. For example, the study might seek to advance knowledge about the exercise habits of American men over the age of 60. In that instance, the "population" is American men over the age of 60. The study might involve collecting data from a scientifically selected *sample* of 2,000 American men over the age of 60. The researchers use statistical techniques to determine whether trends observed in the sample probably exist in the population as well. (If the sample is not scientifically selected, the statistical techniques cannot be used and researchers cannot make inferences about the population.)

2.1.11
probability

Probability is a technical term that refers to the quantifiable likelihood that something will happen, as determined by testable scientific research findings. For example, the probability that a certain brand of computer has a particular defect might be 1 in 1,000, or .001. Do not use *probability* in referring to a person's opinion about the likelihood of something happening. For example, write: "He thinks there is a 90 percent chance that the world will end by the year 2500" —not "a 90 percent probability."

2.1.12
range

The *range* in a set of numbers is the difference between the highest number and the lowest number. For example, if the highest score on a test was 96 and the lowest score was 66, the range was 30.

2.1.13
ratio

A *ratio* refers to the relationship between two numbers. A *ratio* is not a percentage. Write: "Voters approved the referendum by a ratio of 3-to-2" or "Sixty percent of the voters approved the referendum"—not "Voters approved the referendum by a ratio of 60 percent."

2.2 Show that you understand the subtleties of common words and expressions used in describing numbers.

2.2.1
fewer
less

Use *fewer* to refer to items that can be counted. For example, write: "I need to consume fewer calories" —not "I need to consume less calories." Use *less* to modify a singular noun or a predicate adjective, as in "Less snow fell this year" or "She was less enthusiastic than he."

Use *less than* —not *fewer than* —when referring to a measurement of age, money, distance, weight or elapsed time. That is because the quantity involved constitutes an amount, which is considered to be singular. An example of correct usage: "This competition is open to children who are less than 10 years of age."

2.2.2
number
amount

Use *number* in referring to items that are countable, as in "the number of calories in wine." Use *amount* in referring to bulk or mass, as in "the amount of fat in the body."

2.2.3
compose
comprise

The whole *comprises* the parts, and the parts *compose* the whole. Here are examples of correct usage: (1) "The class comprises 10 seniors and five juniors"; (2) "The class consists of 10 seniors and five juniors"; and (3) "The class is composed of 10 seniors and five juniors." Do not use the phrase "comprised of."

2.2.4
compare to
compare with

Use *compare with* when examining differences, as in: "At our university, 770 students are majoring in business this year, compared with 740 last year." Better yet, in that example, write "up from" instead of "compared with." Use *compare to* when likening one thing to another, as in: "This year's football team has been compared to the best teams in school history."

2.2.5
farther
further

Use *farther* in referring to physical distance, as in: "I ran three miles farther that you did." Use *further* to mean "to a greater extent" or "additional."

2.2.6
majority

M*ajority* is considered to be a singular noun when it is not followed by the preposition "of," as in: "The majority has ruled." However, if *majority* is followed by "of," then the object within the "of" phrase determines whether *majority* is singular or plural. For example, you would write "the majority of the Senate is . . ." and "the majority of senators are . . ."

2.2.7
percent

Percent is considered to be a singular noun when it is not followed by the preposition "of," as in: "Ninety percent was an excellent score on that difficult exam." However, if *percent* is followed by "of," then the object within the "of" phrase determines whether *percent* is singular or plural. For example, you would write "70 percent of the Senate is" and "70 percent of the senators are."

2.2.8
data

Data, a plural noun, refers to pieces of information that have been collected or stored, as in: "The questionnaire data were collected last year." Do not use *data* as a singular noun to refer to findings of a statistical analysis, as in: "The data shows . . ." Use an alternative construction such as "the findings show" or "the analysis found."

2.2.9
none

In most instances *none* means "not any" and is considered to be plural. In rare instances *none* can mean "not one," and in those cases *none* is considered to be singular. The word *none* can lead to an awkward-sounding sentence, so the best course is to structure the sentence in such a way that the word *none* need not be used. For example, you could write: "No board officers were re-elected" — not "None of the board officers was/were re-elected."

2.2.10
average

When a particular number is described as being the "average," you need to keep in mind that the word *average* refers to the number — not to the person or organization attached to the number. For example, do not write: "The average American sleeps seven hours a night." Instead, write: "Americans average seven hours of sleep a night."

The word *normal* is not a synonym for *average*. Do not write: "In our city, the normal high temperature for March 20 is 60 degrees." Instead, write: "In our city, the average high temperature for March 20 is 60 degrees." In a particular span of years, 60 degrees might not be the high temperature on any March 20.

2.2.11
another

Another means an additional increment of a similar quantity, as in: "Fifty people registered on

Monday and another 50 registered on Tuesday." It would be incorrect to write: "The fire killed five people and injured another three." The correct construction would be: "The fire killed five people and injured three others." It would be incorrect to write: "The campaign will last another two months." Correct usage is: "The campaign will last two more months."

2.2.12
include

Use the word *include* to indicate that all parts of a whole are not being listed. If all parts of the whole are listed, it is incorrect to use *include*. Here are examples of correct usage: (1) "The seven-member committee consists of three administrators, three faculty members and one student"; and (2) "The seven-member committee includes one student." Do not write: "The seven-member committee includes three administrators, three faculty members and one student."

2.2.13
only

Place the modifier *only* just before the word being modified. For example, write: "I ate only one cookie" — not "I only ate one cookie."

2.2.14
speed

Speed refers to a rate of movement, as in: "The car was traveling at high speed." It is redundant to write: "The car was traveling at a high rate of speed."

2.2.15
zero

Zero refers to a point on a mathematical scale or to the lowest possible score, as in "a temperature of zero degrees" or "a test score of zero." The dictionary acknowledges that *zero* is used in casual speech as an adjective to mean "no" or "not any," but that usage is not considered to be appropriate in formal writing. For example, write: "Diet cola has no calories" — not "Diet cola has zero calories."

2.3 Write clearly.

2.3.1 If you use a subject-and-verb combination early in a sentence, the sentence will be easier to understand. Try to follow what can be called the "8/12 rule": Use a subject within the first eight words of the sentence and a verb within the first 12 words. The eight-word and 12-word spans are narrow enough to force you to focus quickly, yet wide enough to allow you to vary sentence structure. Usually, you will find it easy to use both a subject and a verb within the first 12 words of a sentence.

The subject and verb covered by the 8/12 rule can be: (1) the subject and verb of the sentence; or (2) the subject and verb of a dependent clause that begins the sentence. A dependent clause will begin with a conjunction such as 'if," "unless," "because," "although," "before" or "after."

2.3.2 If a sentence describes an action, normally make the performer of the action the subject of the sentence. That will put the verb in active voice. If you make the receiver of the action the subject of the sentence, the verb will be passive. Active-voice constructions are stronger and usually shorter.

2.3.3 Try to avoid putting more than 35 words in a sentence. Sentences longer than that can be difficult to read. (In your counting, do not include words contained in an attribution phrase at the end of a sentence — a phrase such as "according to a report by the U.S. Environmental Protection Agency.")

2.3.4 When you use a bullet-point vertical list in your writing, make sure that the items listed are parallel in form. For example, you might want to begin each item in the list with the infinitive form of a verb.

2.3.5 Unless you want to be deliberately vague, you should use a precise number or a good estimate whenever you are describing something that is quantifiable. You should avoid vague terms such as these:

- Large
- Small
- Thousands
- Many
- Several
- A lot of
- A few
- Often
- Near

2.3.6 Do not use the term *more than* in trying to provide an estimate, as in: "More than 1,000 people attended." The phrase "more than 1,000" means that the number is between 1,001 and infinity—a useless fact. Use a precise number or an estimate. However, it is appropriate to use "more than" in defining a category, as in: "Five teams won more than 10 games last season."

2.3.7 A *fraction* can range from tiny, such as 1/64, to large, such as 7/8. In expressing a proportion, do not use *fraction* without a modifier such as "tiny" or "large." Better yet, use a more precise term such as "one-tenth" or "10 percent."

2.3.8 The verb "affect" means "to influence" or "to produce a change." If you know how something has been affected or will be affected, use a more precise verb than "affected." For example, write: "Unusually cold weather reduced the company's earnings"—not "affected the company's earnings."

2.5 Write concisely.

2.5.1 Avoid using constructions that lengthen and weaken sentences. For example, write: "We analyzed the data"—not "We did an analysis of the data." Write "Our study aims to . . ."—not "The purpose of our study is to . . ."

2.5.2 Do not use the words "now" or "currently" in stating a number unless you are comparing that number with a number from an earlier time. Write: "Our company has 300 employees"—not "Our company currently has 300 employees."

2.5.3 Do not use these weak, wordy expressions: "positively affected," "negatively affected," "positive effect" or "negative effect." For example, write: "Higher oil prices hurt the company"—not "Higher oil prices negatively affected the company."

2.5.4 Here are examples of redundant expressions to avoid:

five ~~different~~ countries	four ~~separate~~ occasions
~~a total of~~ eight people	~~a distance of~~ two miles
the ~~exact~~ same result	set a ~~new~~ record
each ~~and every~~	every ~~single~~ person

2.5.5 Here are some multi-word expressions that can be replaced by a single word:

Instead of:	*Write:*
a greater number of	more
a lower number of	fewer
due to the fact that	because
pertaining to	about
prior to	before
subsequent to	after

Note

People who want more guidance on writing technique should consult Joseph Keefer's book titled *Zippy Writing: How To Use English Correctly, Clearly and Concisely.*

Section 3

Guidance on Graphics

3.1 Make sure that the information contained in a graphic is correct.

3.1.1 After you have produced a graphic, check your work to make sure that you have not committed careless display errors — errors such as transposing numbers or putting a decimal point in the wrong place.

3.1.2 After you have produced a graphic, check to make sure that the graphic is free of mathematical errors

3.1.3 When you report a sum together with components of that sum, make sure that the components equal the whole. For example, if you state the total U. S. population and the population of each of the four regions of the country, check to confirm that the population of the regions, as stated in your graphic, sums to the total population.

3.1.4 If you report the percentage share of each part of a whole, make sure that the sum of the percentages equals 100 percent — or 99 or 101, accounting for rounding.

3.1.5 If, in your graphic, you display some large numbers in a shortened form, make sure that you correctly indicate what the shortened number represents. For example, if the number "378" in a given column is supposed to be read as "378,000," make sure that the column heading includes the notation "thousands" or "000s."

3.1.6 If you group data into categories for display in a graphic, make sure that the categories are mutually exclusive and collectively exhaustive. Here is an example of a set composed of categories that are neither mutually exclusive nor collectively exhaustive: Group 1—Fewer than 60 points; Group 2—61 through 80 points; and Group 3—80 points and higher.

3.1.7 Be sure to use the correct statistical terminology in the graphic. For example, do not use the term "mean" when the appropriate term is "median," and do not use "percent" when the appropriate term is "percentage-point." Also, in a graphic, do not describe as number being a "total" unless the number is, in fact, a sum of other numbers displayed in the graphic. For example, if, in a table, you list the unemployment rate for each of the states and you want to include a line showing the unemployment rate for the country as a whole, then you should label the overall rate "U. S." — not "Total."

3.2 In a graphic, provide all of the information needed for correct interpretation.

3.2.1 Title the graphic.

3.2.2 Make sure that all columns, rows, axes and other design elements are labeled sufficiently.

3.2.3 Whenever you use a percentage in a graphic, be sure to state the quantity upon which the percentage is based.

3.2.4 If you are describing how two or more groups differ on a particular measure, make sure that your graphic shows the results for all of the groups combined.

3.2.5 If you are reporting results that are based on a randomly selected sample, make sure that your graphic shows the margin of error or another indicator of statistical significance.

3.2.6 At the bottom of the graphic, identify the sources of the data that you used to produce the graphic.

3.2.7 If you are presenting research findings in an academic journal or at an academic conference, make sure to provide graphics at the prescribed level of detail and in the prescribed format.

3.3 Avoid producing graphics that can mislead readers.

3.3.1 If you are using a vertical bar chart to show differences between positive-integer percentages or quantities, you should base the vertical axis at zero. Using a base other than zero can result in a misleading graphic, with readers overestimating how much groups differ on certain measures. (See Examples 1A and 1B, page 58.)

3.3.2 If you are using a horizontal bar chart to show differences between positive-integer percentages or quantities, you should base the horizontal axis at zero. Using a base other than zero can result in a misleading graphic. (See Examples 2A and 2B, page 59.)

3.3.3 If negative-integer percentages or quantities are involved, you should use a vertical bar chart and base the vertical axis at a point just below the lowest value. (See Example 6B, page 63). Do not use a horizontal bar chart if negative-integer percentages are involved.

3.3.4 If you are using a line chart to show how a particular measure has changed over time, you can safely base the vertical axis at a number higher than zero if, historically, value of the measure has never been zero. In such a circumstance, the axis would begin at a point just below the lowest value and would end at a point just above the highest value. (See Example 13A, page 69).

3.3.5 You should avoid using pictographs—those symbols that depict objects such as cars or houses. Using the relative size of pictographs to show statistical differences between groups can end up causing readers to overestimate those differences. (In addition, pictographs are distracting.)

3.3.6 You should avoid using three-dimensional bars to display two-dimensional data in your charts. Displaying bars in three dimensions can lead readers to overestimate statistical differences between groups.

3.4 Structure graphics in ways that make major statistical findings easy to discern.

3.4.1 Guard against putting so much information in a graphic that the main point you are trying to make is obscured.

For example:

• In a statistical table, try to avoid displaying more than six columns of data.

• In a vertical bar chart, try to avoid using more than six categories on the horizontal axis.

• In a line chart, try to avoid graphing more than six lines of data.

3.4.2 One type of table can be used to show how, at certain points in time, various categories differ in quantity and in percentage of a whole. In a table like that, you should arrange the quantity columns side-by-side and the percentage columns side-by-side, which makes the numbers easier to compare. (See Examples 3A and 3B, page 60).

3.4.3 Sometimes a researcher is analyzing how similar entities vary on a particular measure—for example, how the four U. S. geographic regions differ in the size of their population. In tables of that type, you should list the entities in descending rank order based on the major variable being analyzed, and you should display the ranking variable in the far right column. (See Examples 3A and 3B, page 60).

3.4.4 A crosstabulation table is used in examining the relationship between two categorical variables. In a crosstabulation table, you should display the categories of the independent variable across the top of the table and the categories of the dependent variable down the left side of the table. (See Example 4, page 61).

3.4.5 A scatterplot is used to depict the relationship between two continuous variables. In a scatterplot, you need to place the independent variable on the horizontal axis and the dependent variable on the vertical axis. Use tick marks on each axis. (See Example 5, page 62).

3.4.6 If you are using a vertical bar chart in which categories of data are displayed on the horizontal axis, you normally should present the categories left-to-right in descending rank order if you want to emphasize the highest-value category. (See Examples 6A and 6B, page 63). However, if you want to emphasize the lowest-value category because "lower is better," then you normally should present the categories left-to-right in ascending rank order.

3.4.7 If you are using a vertical bar chart in which the horizontal axis is delineated in years—such as 2014, 2015 and 2016—then you should display the vertical bars in a sequence that places the earliest year on the left.

3.4.8 Normally, a vertical bar chart is easier to read than a horizontal bar chart. However, a horizontal bar chart is better if: (1) a variable being analyzed has many categories; or (2) the category labels are long. (See Example 2B, page 59).

3.4.9 If you are using a horizontal bar chart, you should display the categories top-down in descending rank order, assuming that you want to emphasize the highest-value category. (See Example 2B, page 59). However, if you want to emphasize the lowest-value category, then you should display the categories top-down in ascending rank order.

3.4.10 In some tables and charts, readers expect to see categories listed sequentially in a standardized order—not in rank order. As one example, "marital status" usually has several categories, beginning with "married" and ending with "never married." As another example, a "satisfaction scale" usually has several categories, beginning with "very dissatisfied" and ending with "very satisfied." In tables like those, you should display the categories in the standardized order.

3.4.11 You should avoid using pie charts or doughnut charts. Data can be displayed more clearly in tables and bar charts than in pie charts or doughnut charts.

3.5 In your graphics, make the text, numbers and design elements easy to read.

3.5.1 Use a white background for tables and charts that will be displayed in print.

3.5.2 In graphics for print, do not use type smaller than 10 point.

3.5.3 Use a white or beige background for slides presented in a conference-room setting.

3.5.4 Use a blue background and white or yellow text for slides presented in a large-room setting.

3.5.5 In graphics for slides, do not use type smaller than 18 point.

3.5.6 In graphics for slides, use a sans-serif font such as Arial, in contrast to a serif font such as Times Roman.

3.5.7 When developing a slide presentation, make sure that all elements on all slides are clear enough to be read by everyone in the audience.

3.5.8 In graphics for print or slides, do not use italicized text or all-capitals text.

3.5.9 Try to avoid using slanted or rotated text in displaying labels in a table or in a bar chart or in a line chart. (See Examples 7A and 7B, page 64.) However, in a scatterplot, it is customary to use rotated text in labeling the vertical axis.

3.5.10 In a horizontal bar chart, you should place the horizontal axis above the chart. (See Example 2B, page 59.)

3.5.11 Avoid having wide gaps between columns in tables and avoid having wide gaps between bars in charts.

3.5.12 In graphics for print or slides, you should avoid using a long unpunctuated string of numbers to express an amount. If a precise amount needs to be stated, then write, for example, 49,733,422 — not 49733422.

3.5.13 Try to avoid labeling a column in a table in a way that forces readers to visualize a number that is a thousand times larger than the number displayed. For example, if you labeled a column "in thousands," the reader would need to view the number 2,615 as meaning 2,615,000, or 2.615 million. Simply label the column "in millions" and use "2.6."

3.5.14 If, in a table, you need to express a per-centage that is less than 1, place a zero to the left of the decimal point for the sake of clarity. For example, display "0.3 percent" — not ".3 percent."

3.5.15 When, within a table, you display a column of whole numbers, you should format the column so that the numbers are right-aligned vertically and are centered horizontally. Here are examples:

Incorrect	Incorrect	Correct
1,054	1,054	1,054
765	765	765
648	648	648

3.5.16 When, within a table, you display a column of numbers containing a decimal point, you should format the column so that the numbers are lined up on the decimal point. Thus, you might need to add a ".0" to one or more numbers. Here are examples:

Incorrect	Incorrect	Correct
42.7%	42.7%	42.7%
31%	31%	31.0%
26.3%	26.3%	26.3%

3.5.17 If rows in a table display years and related data, place the most recent year at the top. Here is an example:

49

U. S. population, by year

2015 (Estimate)	321,418,820
2010 (Census)	308,745,538
2000 (Census)	281,421,906

3.5.18 If columns in a table are labeled by year, place the earliest year on the left. Here is an example:

Population of the three largest states

	2000	2010	2015
California	33,871,648	37,253,956	39,144,818
Texas	20,851,820	25,145,561	27,469,114
Florida	15,982,378	18,801,310	20,271,272

3.5.19 Bright colors can be hard on the eyes, so, in color bar charts you should fill the bars with colors that are subtle yet differentiating.

3.5.20 If you are displaying only one data series in a full-size black-white-and-gray chart, you should fill the bars with a medium shade of gray instead of black. (See Examples 6A and 6B, page 63.) A full-size chart dominated by black bars can be hard on the eyes. However, if you need to submit a small-scale version of your chart for inclusion in a publication, you should color the bars black in that version.

3.5.21 Whenever you produce a document or a presentation that includes color graphics, you should also prepare a version in black, white and gray for people who want to print a black-and-white version. Color graphics that are printed in black and white can be confusing.

3.6 Avoid cluttering your graphics with numbers that readers do not need.

3.6.1 In a table or a chart, you should round large amounts to the level that seems logical. For example, if all numbers being displayed in a table column are between $1 million and $10 million, then shorten the numbers to a whole number and one decimal place and indicate "in millions" atop the column. (For example, $1,685,467 would be displayed as "$1.7.") When reporting large amounts, you should use the precise number only if you think readers might expect that level of detail.

3.6.2 Do not display more than one decimal unit with a percentage shown in a table or a chart unless small differences are important or unless additional decimal units are prescribed by the entity that is evaluating or using your research. Often, you can simply round percentages to the nearest whole.

3.6.3 If an axis on a chart consists only of whole numbers, as is usually the case, do not display a ".0" or a ".00" after the number. (See Examples 7A and 7B, page 64.)

3.6.4 In a crosstabulation table, there is usually no need to state the number of people represented by the various percentages. However, you do need to make sure to state the quantity upon which the percentages are based. (See Example 4, page 61.)

3.7 Avoid cluttering your graphics with distracting or unnecessary design elements.

3.7.1 In a chart, place the same "fill color" in each bar within a series of bars displaying differences between categories on a particular variable. Coloring the bars differently can confuse readers. (See Examples 7A and 7B, page 64.)

3.7.2 If you are producing a bar chart that will be displayed in black, white and gray, find ways to use "solid fills" to differentiate the bars. Do not use "fill patterns" within the bars of a chart. (See Examples 7A and 7B, page 64.)

3.7.3 Whenever possible, you should avoid using a legend in a chart. Instead, place labels directly on the bars or lines being used to display data. (See Examples 8A and 8B, on page 65, Examples 9A and 9B on page 66, and Examples 10A and 10B on page 67.) If you cannot avoid using a legend, center it near the bottom of the chart.

3.7.4 Horizontal gridlines can be useful in a vertical bar chart or in a line chart, but make sure that you use only faint lines. (See Examples 7A and 7B, page 64.)

3.7.5 In a horizontal bar chart, do not display an axis line on either axis. (See Example 2B, page 59.)

3.7.6 In a vertical bar chart, do not display an axis line on the vertical axis. (See Examples 8A and 8B, page 65.)

3.7.7 In a vertical bar chart or a line chart, you should display an axis line on the horizontal axis if you use gridlines in the chart. Make the axis line the same thickness as the gridlines. If gridlines are not used in the chart, do not display an axis line on the horizontal axis. (See Examples 8A and 8B, page 65, and Examples 9A and 9B, page 66.)

3.7.8 Do not use tick marks on either axis of a bar chart. (See Examples 8A and 8B, page 65.)

3.7.9 In a line chart, do not display an axis line or tick marks on the vertical axis. (See Examples 10A and 10B, page 67.)

3.7.10 In most circumstances, tick marks are not needed on the horizontal axis of a line chart. If tick marks are used on the horizontal axis, they should be of the same thickness as the horizontal gridlines and they should be placed on the outside of the axis line.

3.7.11 If you are producing a line chart that will be displayed in black, white and gray, find ways to use "solid fills" to differentiate the lines. Do not use dotted lines or dashed lines. (See Examples 10A and 10B, page 67.)

3.7.12 If you want to use "marker shapes" in a line chart, use only the shape of a dot and avoid other shapes such as a square or a triangle. (See Examples 10A and 10B, page 67.)

3.7.13 In a table, you should not normally display the name of a variable if the variable name is obvious or can be inferred from the title of the table. For example, if four rows within a column list the names of the four U. S. geographic regions, there is no reason to label the column "region." However, if you are presenting a complex table involving a series of independent variables, you should display the name of each of the variables for the sake of consistency.

3.7.14 In a chart, you should not title an axis if the name of the variable being displayed on the axis is obvious or can be inferred from the title of the chart. For example, if a horizontal axis displays the numbers 2014, 2015 and 2016, there is no reason to title the axis as "year."

3.7.15 In most tables or in a chart, you should not use a percent sign after a number if the title of the graphic or other text makes it clear that the number is a percentage. However, in a cross-tabulation table, it makes sense to use the percent sign after numbers for the sake of clarity.

3.7.16 You should avoid using a currency symbol, such as a dollar sign, in front of a number if it is clear that the number is an amount of money.

3.7.17 If a bar chart or a line chart displays only one data series, you can directly label the data points, eliminating the need for numbers on the data axis and eliminating any need for gridlines. (See Examples 11 and 12, page 68, and Example 13B, page 69.) If the chart displays more than one data series, you should avoid directly labeling data points.

3.7.18 Do not display gridlines within a table. (See Examples 14A and 14B, page 70.)

3.7.19 Do not display a box around a graphic unless the graphic is a scatterplot or unless the graphic needs to be set apart from adjacent text on a page within a document.

Note

The guidance contained in Section 3 reflects the author's views about what constitutes "best practices" in the design of statistical graphics. If you receive different guidance on a particular point of design style from the entity that is evaluating or using your research, you should, of course, follow the guidance offered by that entity.

**Examples of statistical graphics
are presented on pages 58 through 70.**

Notes

(1) All of the statistics displayed in the following examples of tables and charts are genuine.

(2) To save space, the example graphics do not show data sources and other supplemental information that would need to be included in any graphic that is prepared for publication.

(3) Boldface text was used throughout the example graphics to make the graphics easier to read in this narrow-book format. Typically, boldface is used only for headings in graphics.

(4) To keep down the cost of this book, color graphics were not used. Color is not necessary for illustrating the principles of good design described in Section 3.

Example 1A: A misleading chart

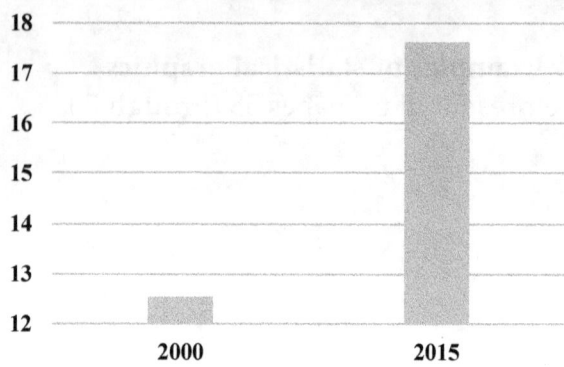

**Hispanics' percentage share
of the U. S. population**

Example 1B: An improved version of the chart

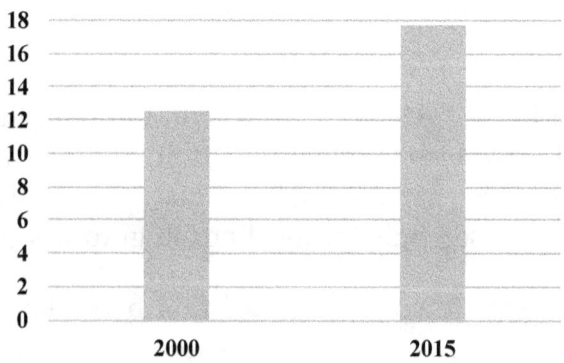

**Hispanics' percentage share
of the U. S. population**

Example 2A: A misleading chart

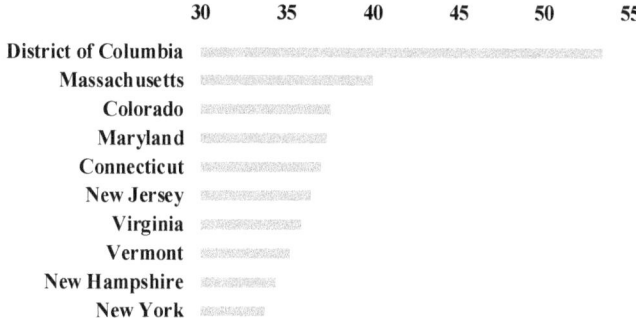

Top 10 states in percentage of the adult population
with a college degree

Example 2B: An improved version of the chart

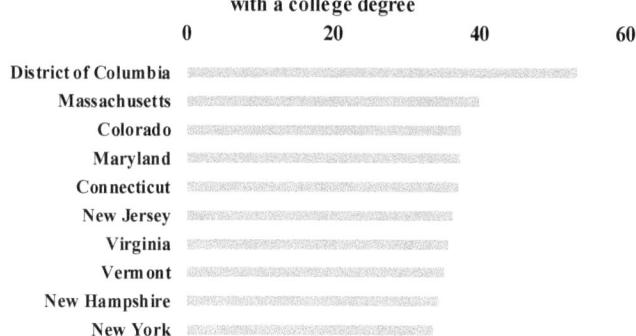

Top 10 states in percentage of the adult population
with a college degree

Example 3A: A table that needs to be improved

U. S. population, by region

| | 2000 | | 2015 | |
	Population (Census)	Pct. share of U. S. population	Population (Estimated)	Pct. share of U. S. population
Northeast	53,594,810	19.0	56,283,891	17.5
Midwest	64,396,653	22.9	67,907,403	21.1
South	100,234,523	35.6	121,182,847	37.7
West	63,198,614	22.5	76,044,679	23.7
Total	281,424,600		321,418,820	

Example 3B: An improved version of the table

U. S. population, by region

| | Population | | Pct. share of U. S. population | |
	2000 (Census)	2015 (Estimated)	2000	2015
South	100,234,523	121,182,847	35.6	37.7
West	63,198,614	76,044,679	22.5	23.7
Midwest	64,396,653	67,907,403	22.9	21.1
Northeast	53,594,810	56,283,891	19.0	17.5
Total	281,424,600	321,418,820		

Example 4

**Political party preference, by sex,
among Americans interviewed
in the 2014 General Social Survey**

	Men	Women	Overall
Democrat	**29.2%**	**35.8%**	**32.8%**
Republican	**23.5%**	**19.7%**	**21.4%**
Independent	**44.1%**	**42.7%**	**43.3%**
Other parties	**3.2%**	**1.9%**	**2.5%**
Number of respondents	**1,129**	**1,383**	**2,512**

Example 5

The relationship between exercise and obesity

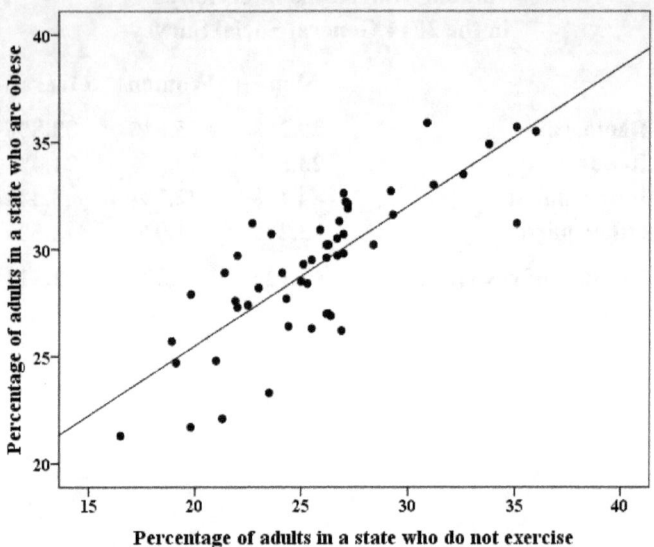

Note: In this scatterplot, a symbol represents a state.

Example 6A: A chart that needs to be improved

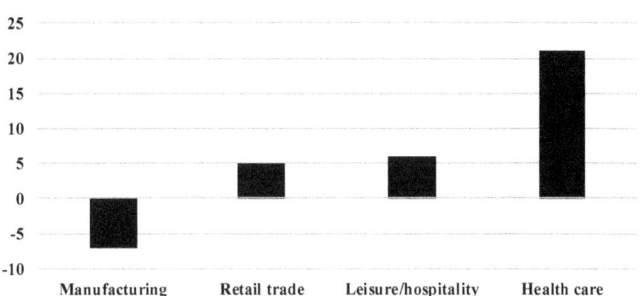

Projected percentage change in the number of jobs within selected U. S. industry sectors between 2014 and 2024

Example 6B: An improved version of the chart

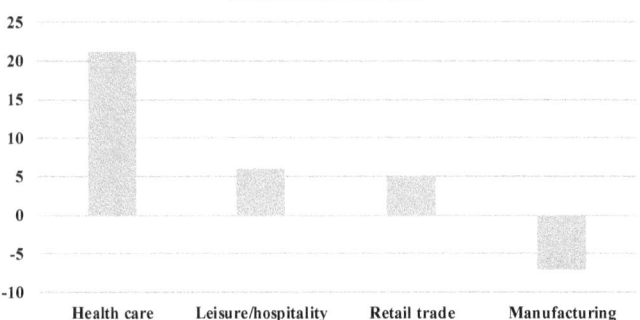

Projected percentage change in the number of jobs within selected U. S. industry sectors between 2014 and 2024

Example 7A: A chart that needs to be improved

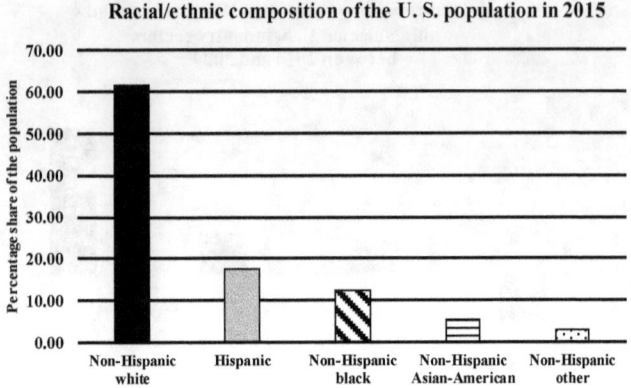

Example 7B: An improved version of the chart

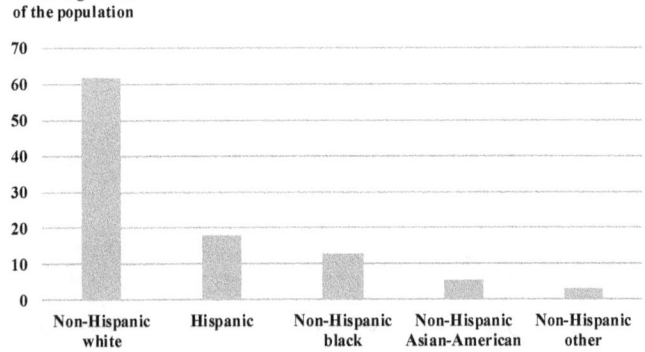

Example 8A: A chart that needs to be improved

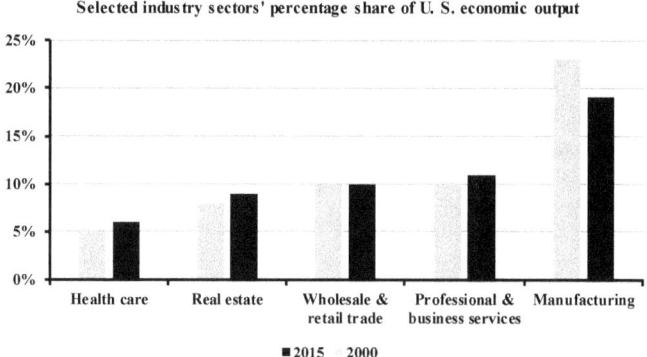

Example 8B: An improved version of the chart

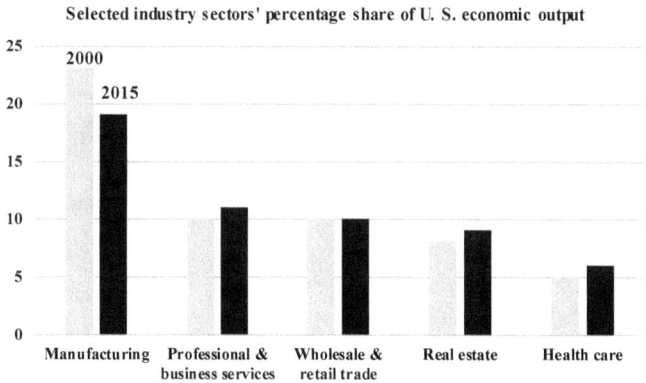

Example 9A: A chart that needs to be improved

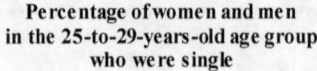

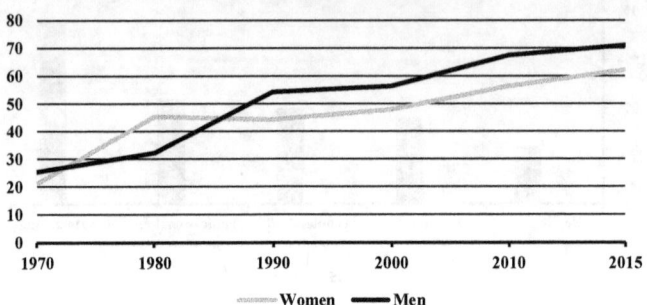

Example 9B: An improved version of the chart

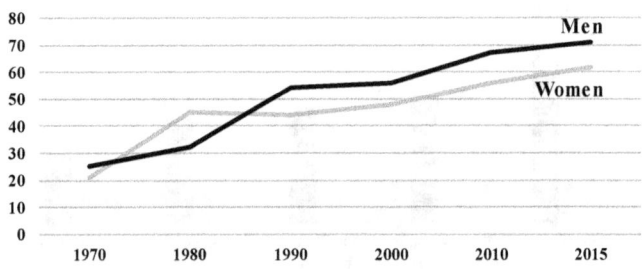

Example 10A: A chart that needs to be improved

Selected countries' percentage share of the total value of goods imported into the U. S.

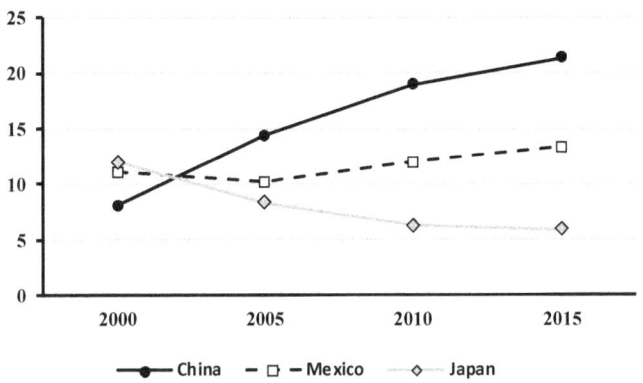

Example 10B: An improved version of the chart

Selected countries' percentage share of the total value of goods imported into the U. S.

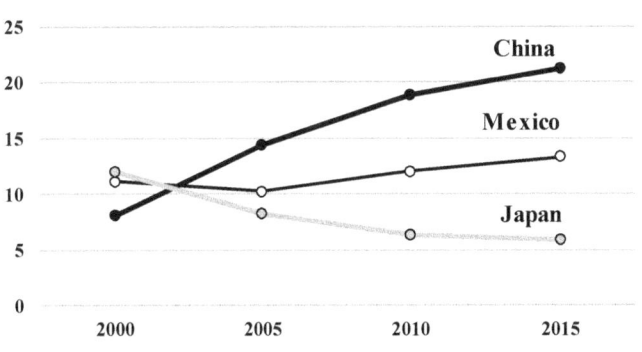

Example 11

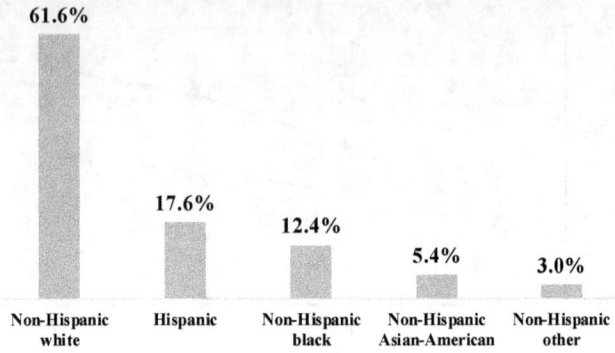

Racial/ethnic composition of the U. S. population in 2015

Note: Hispanics can be of any race.

Example 12

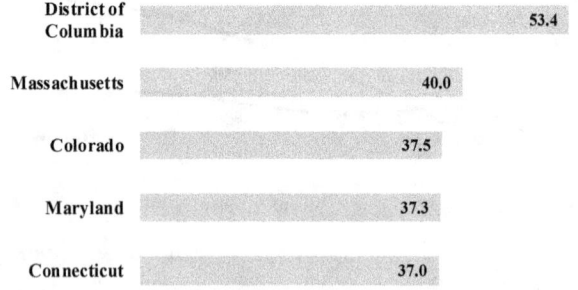

**Top five states in percentage of the adult population
with a college degree in 2015**

Example 13A

**Population of the United States
(in millions)**

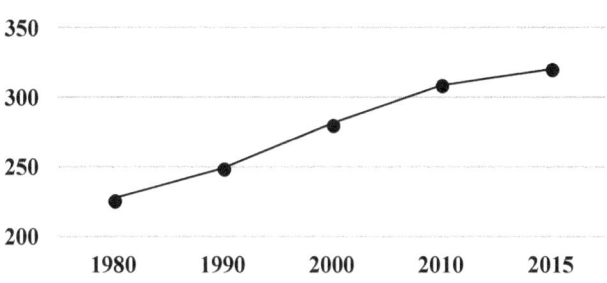

Example 13B

**Population of the United States
(in millions)**

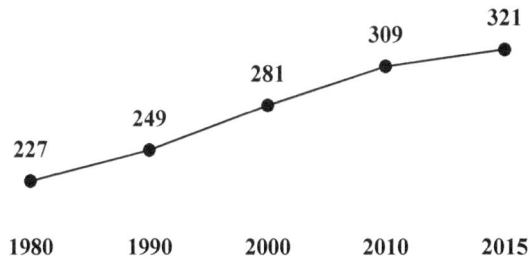

Example 14A: A table that needs to be improved

Projected U. S. population growth between 2015 and 2030, by age group

	Estimated 2015 population (in millions)	Projected 2030 population (in millions)	Projected growth Number (in millions)	Pct.
Under 18 years	73.6	76.3	2.7	3.7%
18-64 years	200.0	209.0	9.0	4.5%
65 years and over	47.8	74.1	26.3	55.0%
Total	321.4	359.4	38.0	11.8%

Example 14B: An improved version of the table

Projected U. S. population growth between 2015 and 2030, by age group

	Estimated 2015 population (in millions)	Projected 2030 population (in millions)	Projected growth Number (in millions)	Pct.
Under 18 years	73.6	76.3	2.7	3.7%
18-64 years	200.0	209.0	9.0	4.5%
65 years and over	47.8	74.1	26.3	55.0%
Total	321.4	359.4	38.0	11.8%

Joseph D. Keefer

Joseph D. Keefer is director of the Center for Excellence in English Usage, based in Chapel Hill, North Carolina. He is also an independent consultant specializing in communicating quantitative information.

Keefer's varied career has included service as:

- An associate professor of communications at Penn State University

- An associate professor of social sciences at Zayed University in Dubai and Abu Dhabi

- A senior-level staff assistant to Congressman Walter Flowers in the U. S. House of Representatives

- Chief lobbyist for the Council on Alternate Fuels, a Washington, D. C.-based trade association

- A policy analyst for the Iowa Utilities Board

- A copy editor for *The Columbus Dispatch*

- A copy editor for *The Des Moines Register*

- A reporter and editor for United Press International

- A reporter and editor for McGraw-Hill Publications

Keefer has written five books aimed at helping students and professionals communicate better in words and numbers.

Keefer holds a Ph.D. in mass communication research from the University of North Carolina at Chapel Hill, an M.A. in international communication from The Ohio State University and a B.A. in journalism from Ohio State.

Books About Words and Numbers
By
Joseph D. Keefer

Classy Stats:
How To Communicate
Quantitative Information Effectively

Spell-Checker Follies:
Guidance on Avoiding
Word-Choice Blunders

The Pro's English:
A Guide for Meeting the Highest Standards
Of Word Usage

Zippy Writing:
How To Use English
Correctly, Clearly and Concisely

Urgent English:
A Guide to the English Usage Basics
That You Need To Know